DREAM FLORA

AN ADULT COLORING BOOK

Victoria Wilchcombe

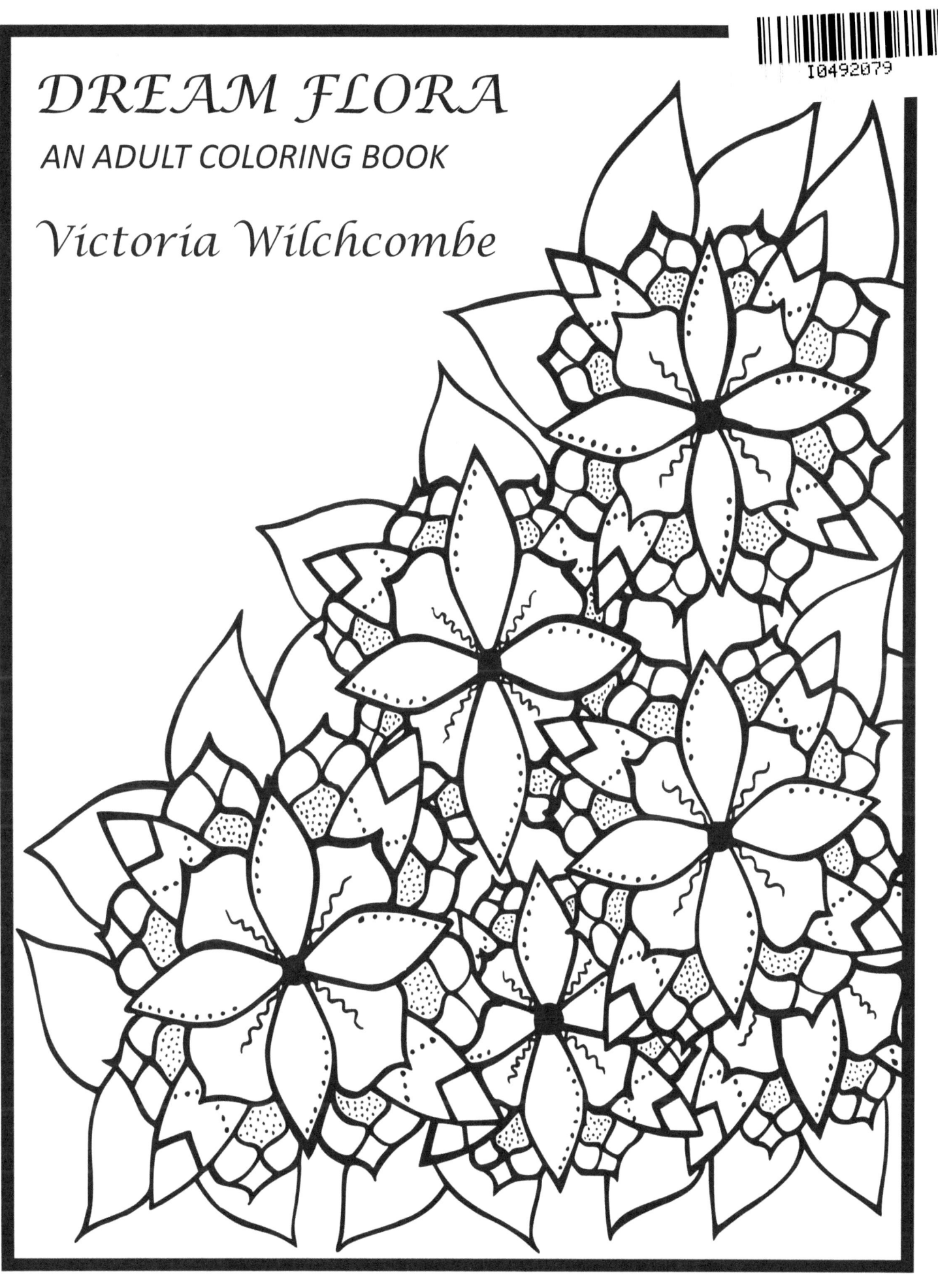

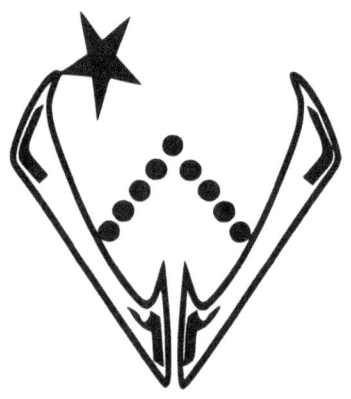

This book belongs to:

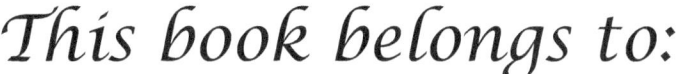

FROM THE AUTHOR

I have always viewed flowers as a master work of art and have been sketching flower patterns since I was kid. I am forever grateful that you decided to purchase Dream Flora; it truly means the world to me.

If you enjoyed my art you will be happy to know that I am working on two more coloring books for this series but with a twist. I hope to have them released by mid-year.

P.S. I think framing your favorites is an awesome idea and would surely be eye-catching.

Yours Truly,
Victoria

Follow me on twitter @starbeam88 for updates and a look at my other projects.

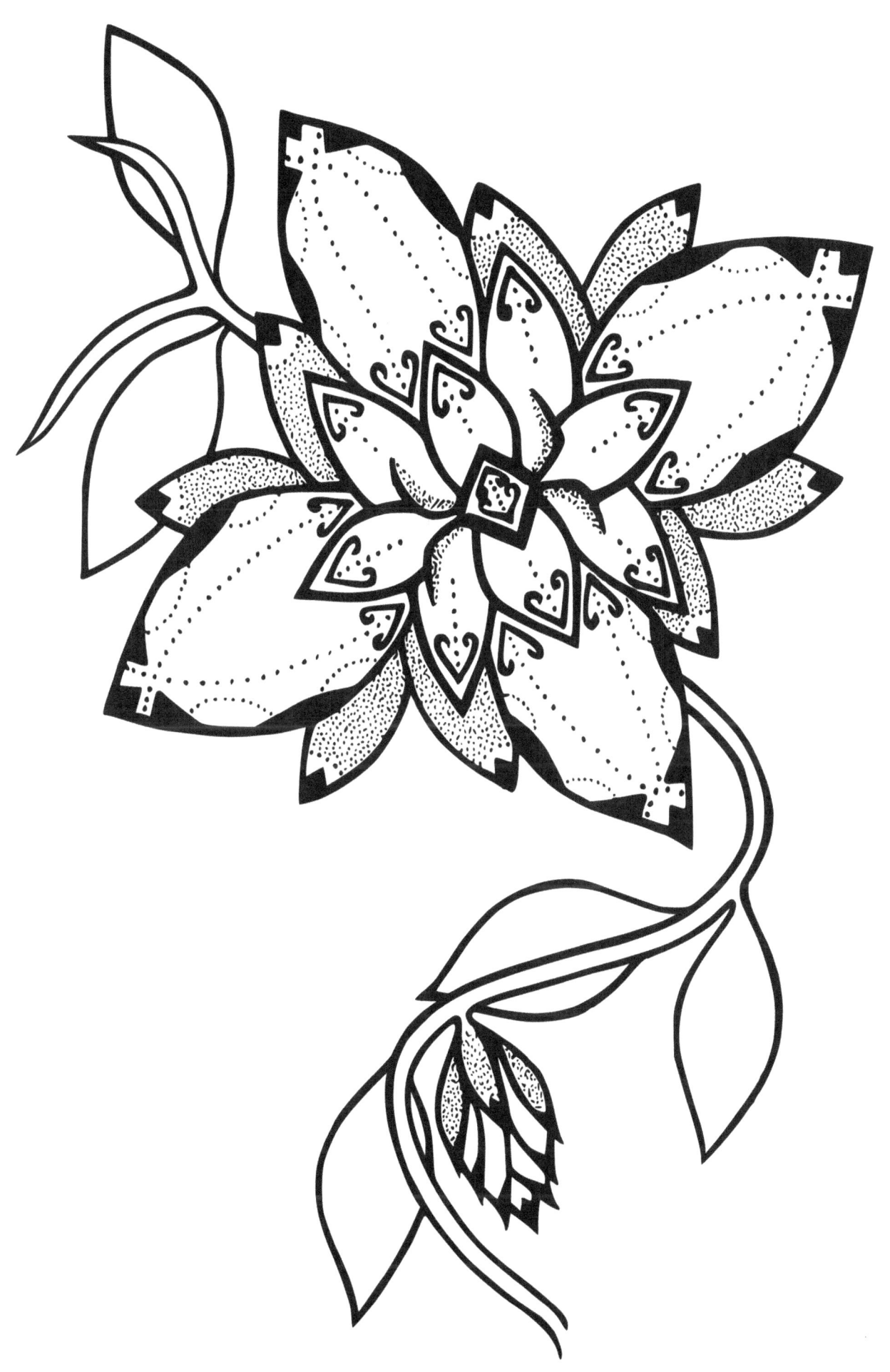

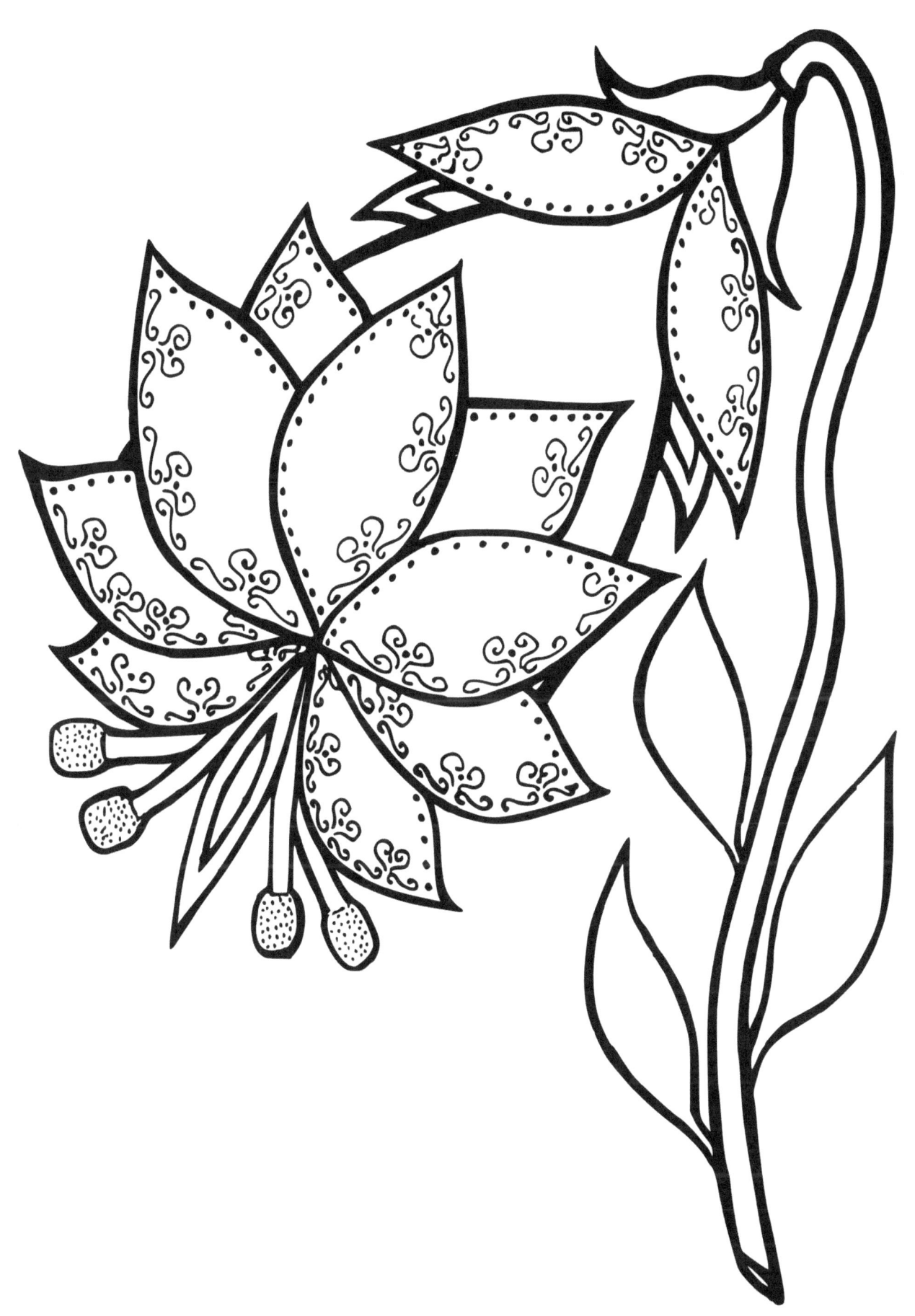

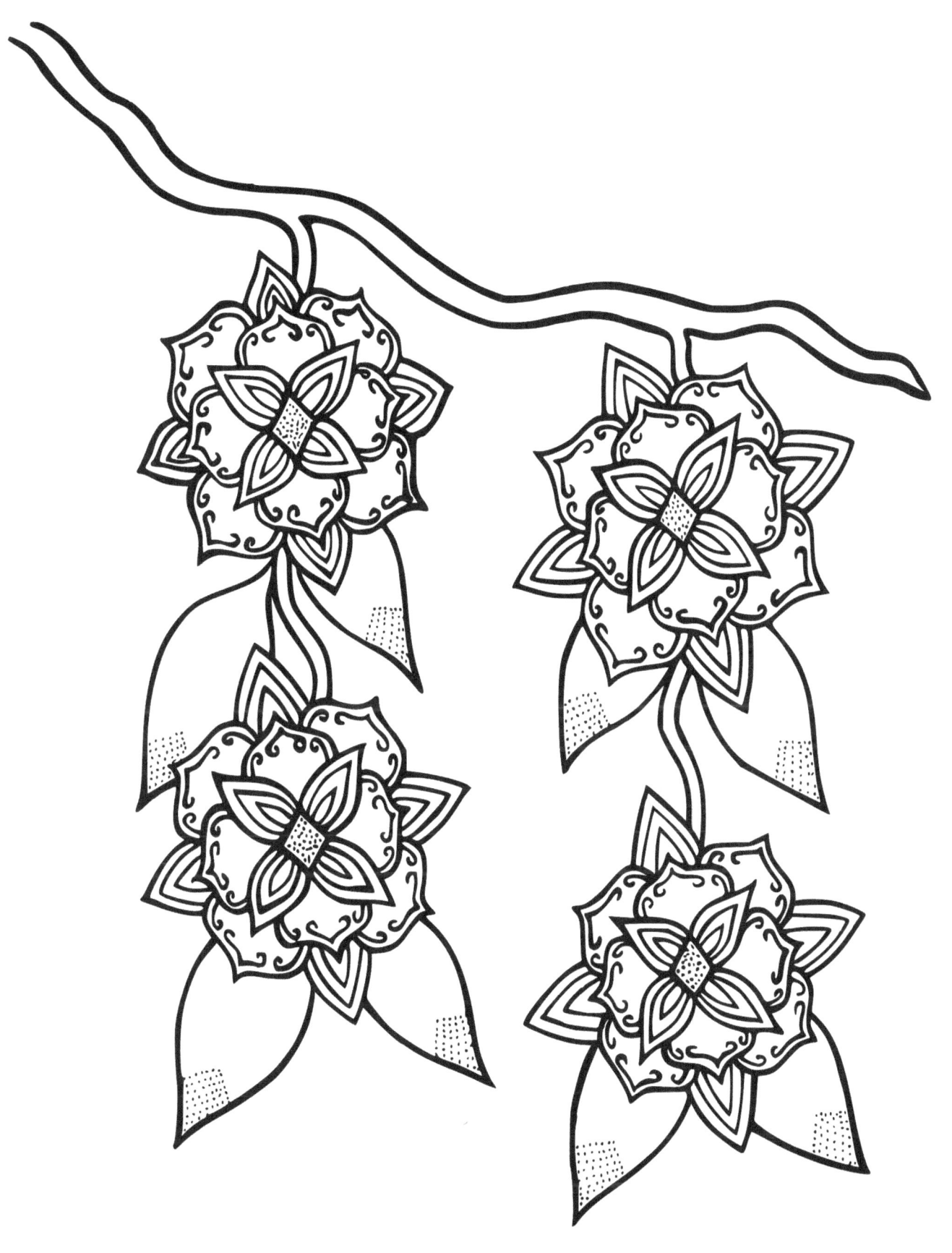

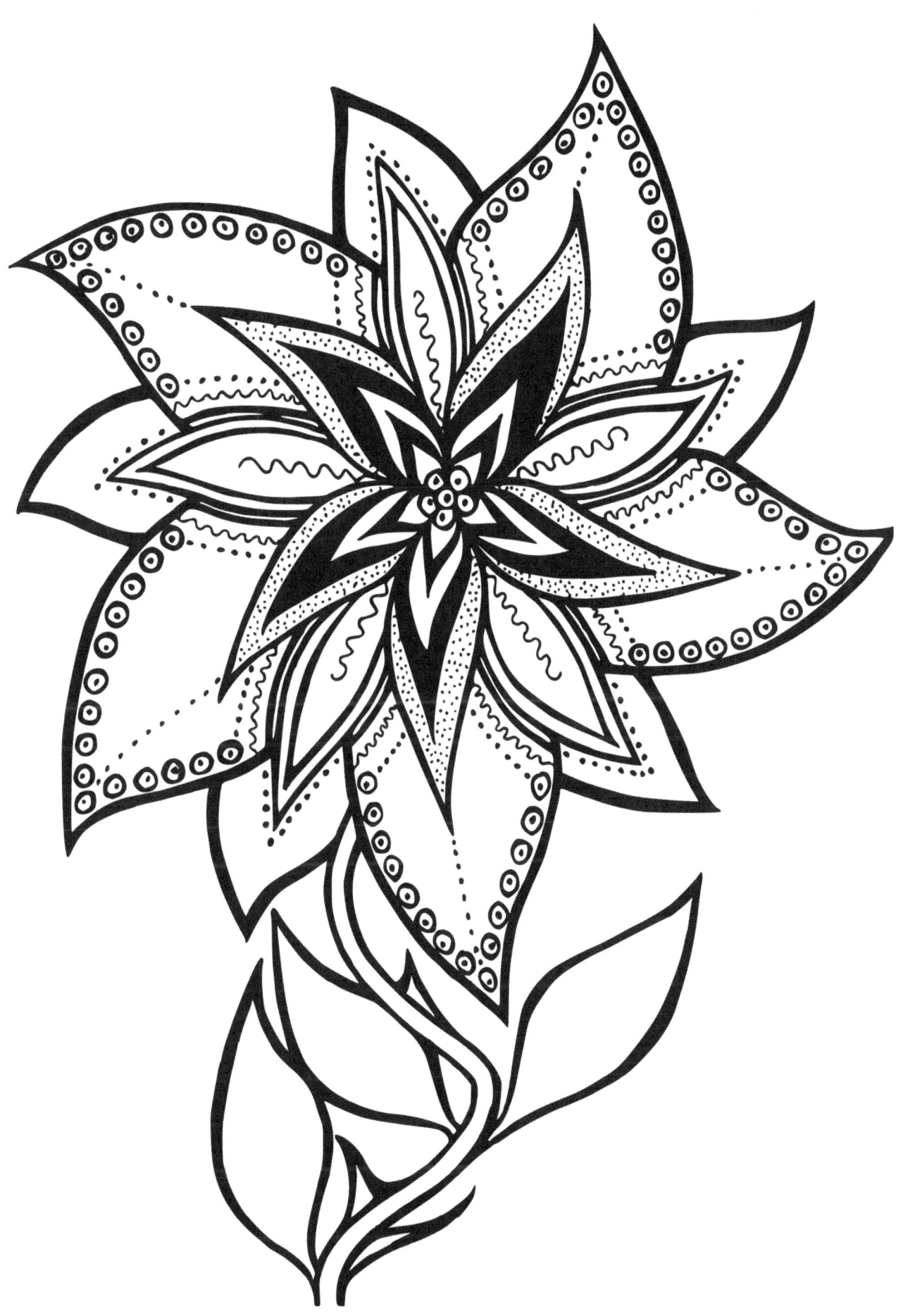

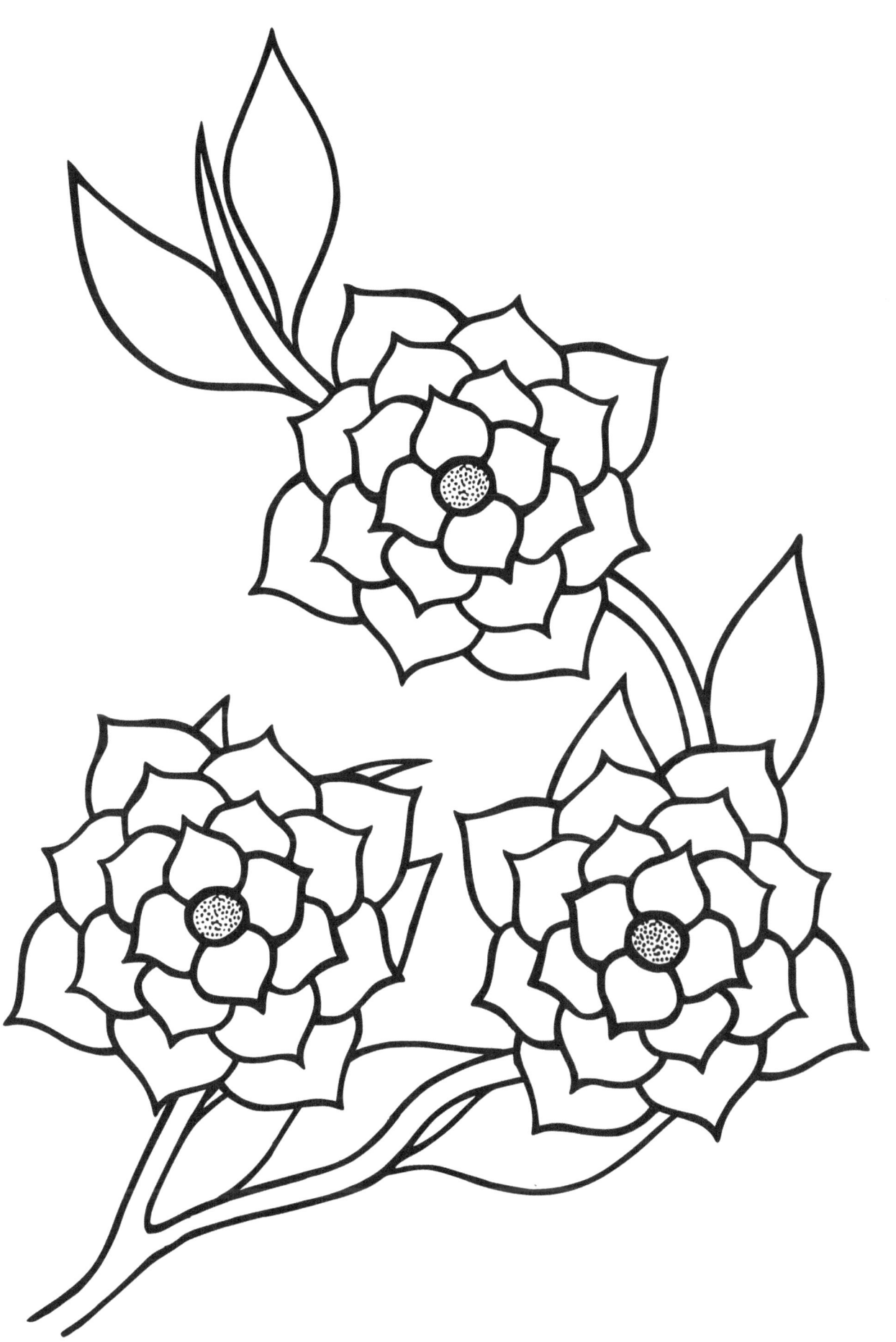

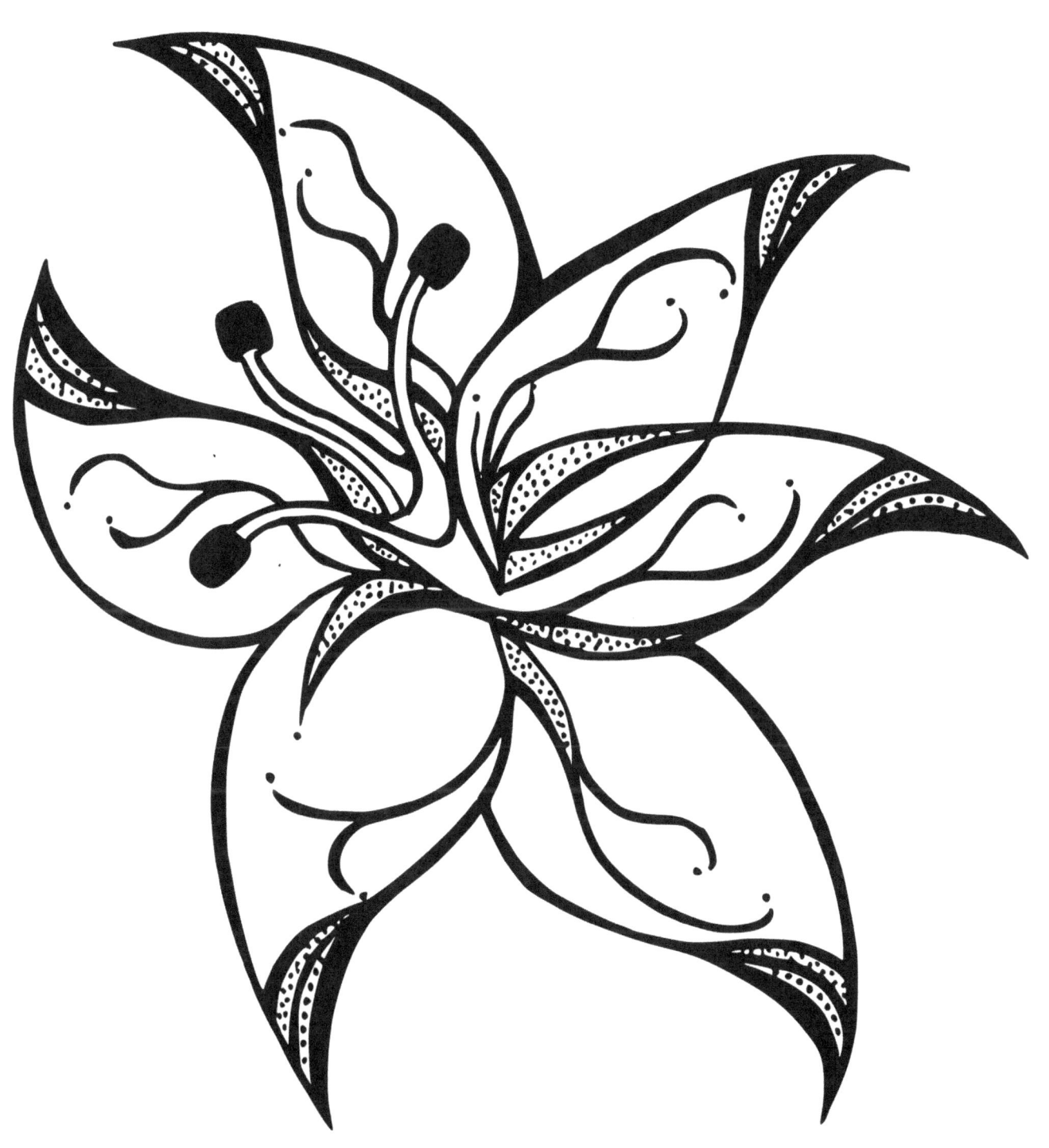

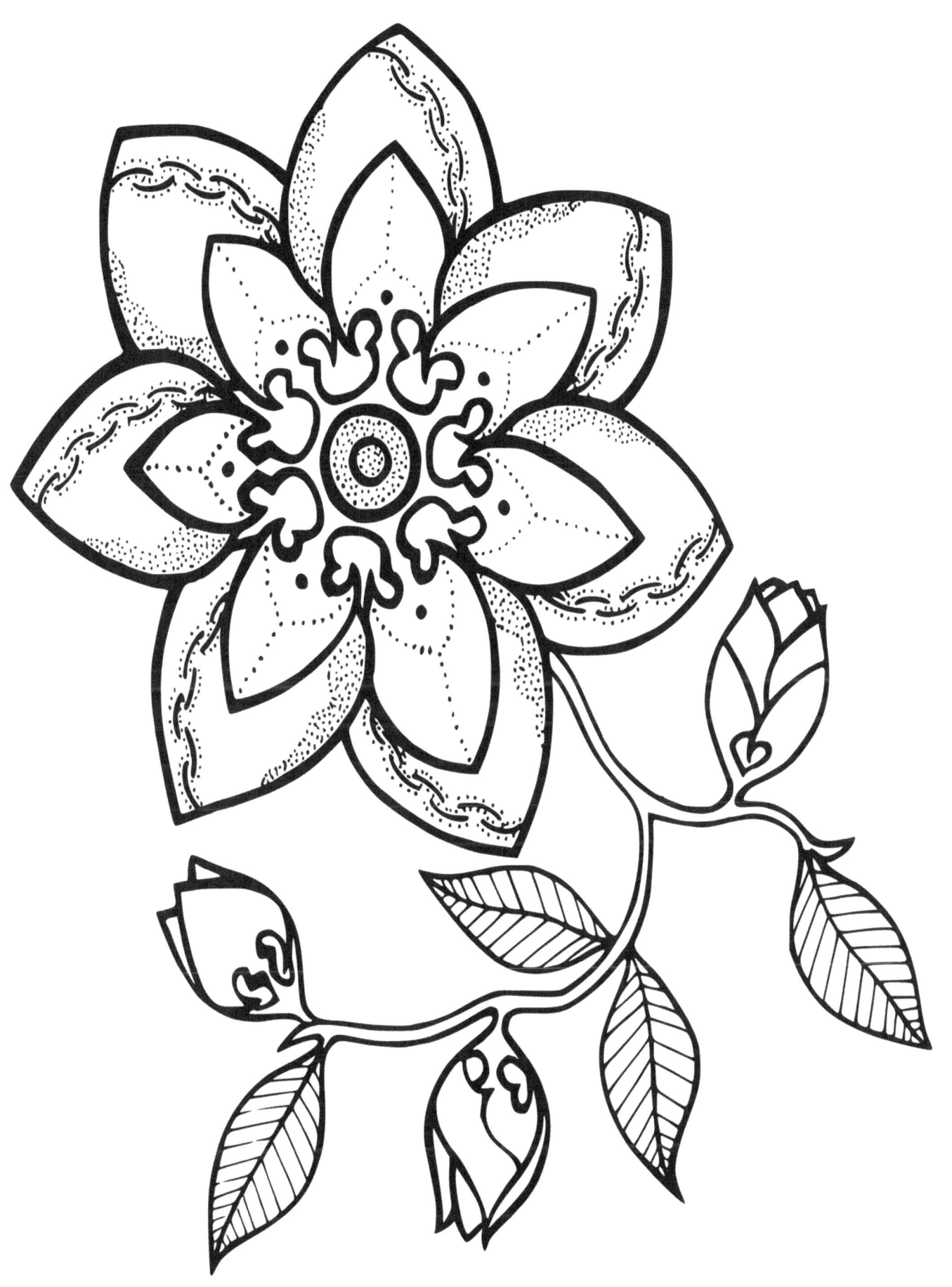

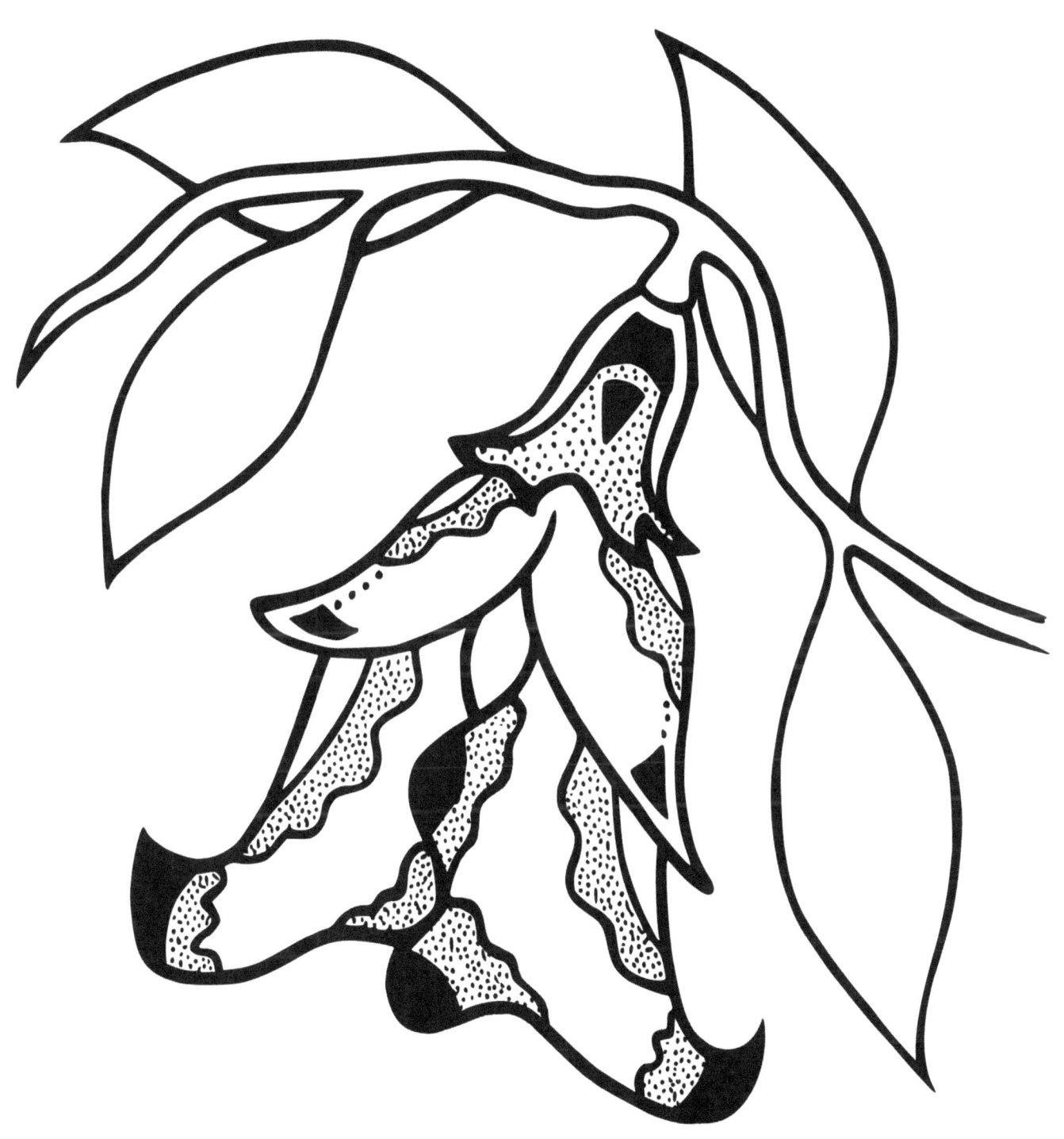

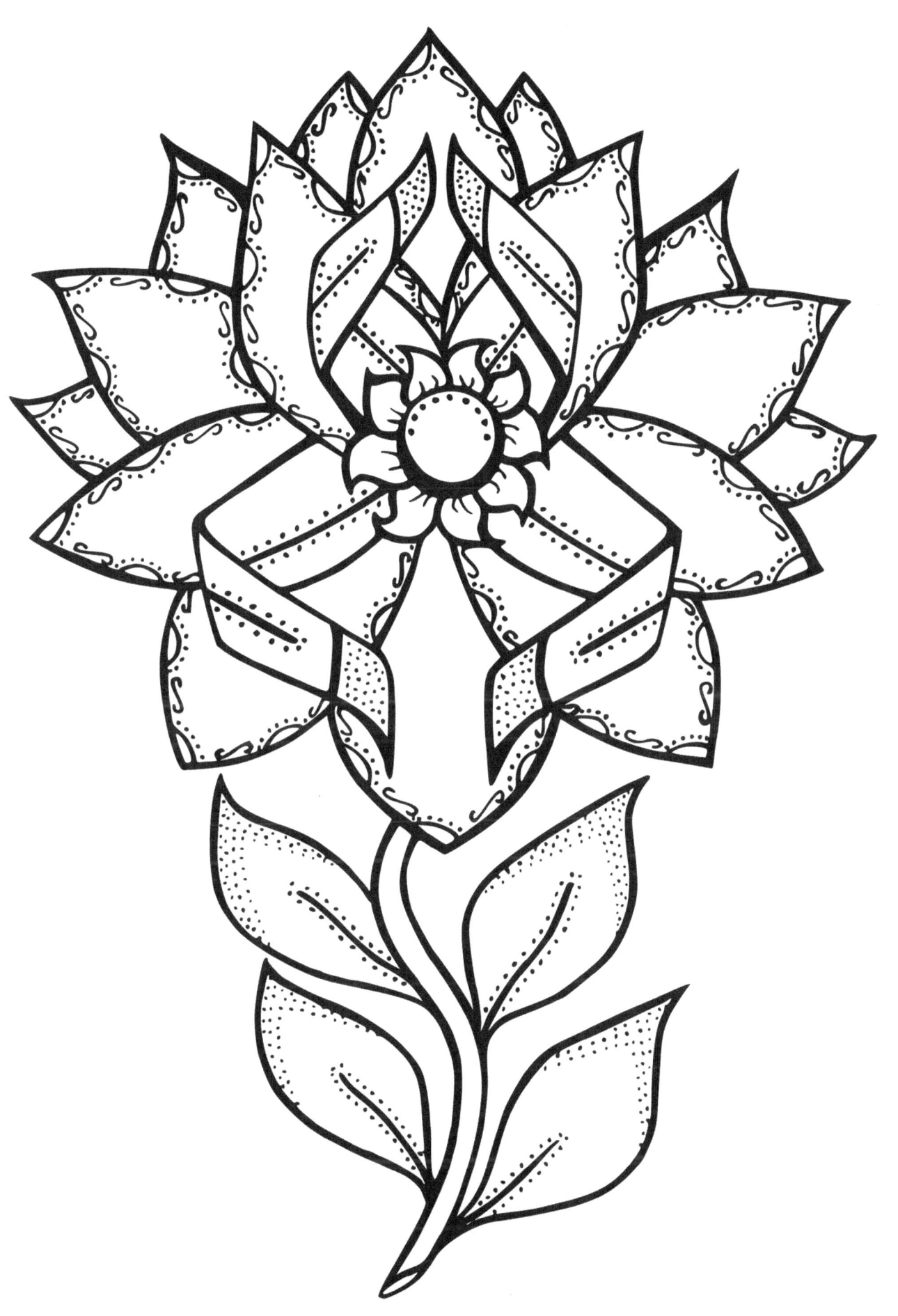

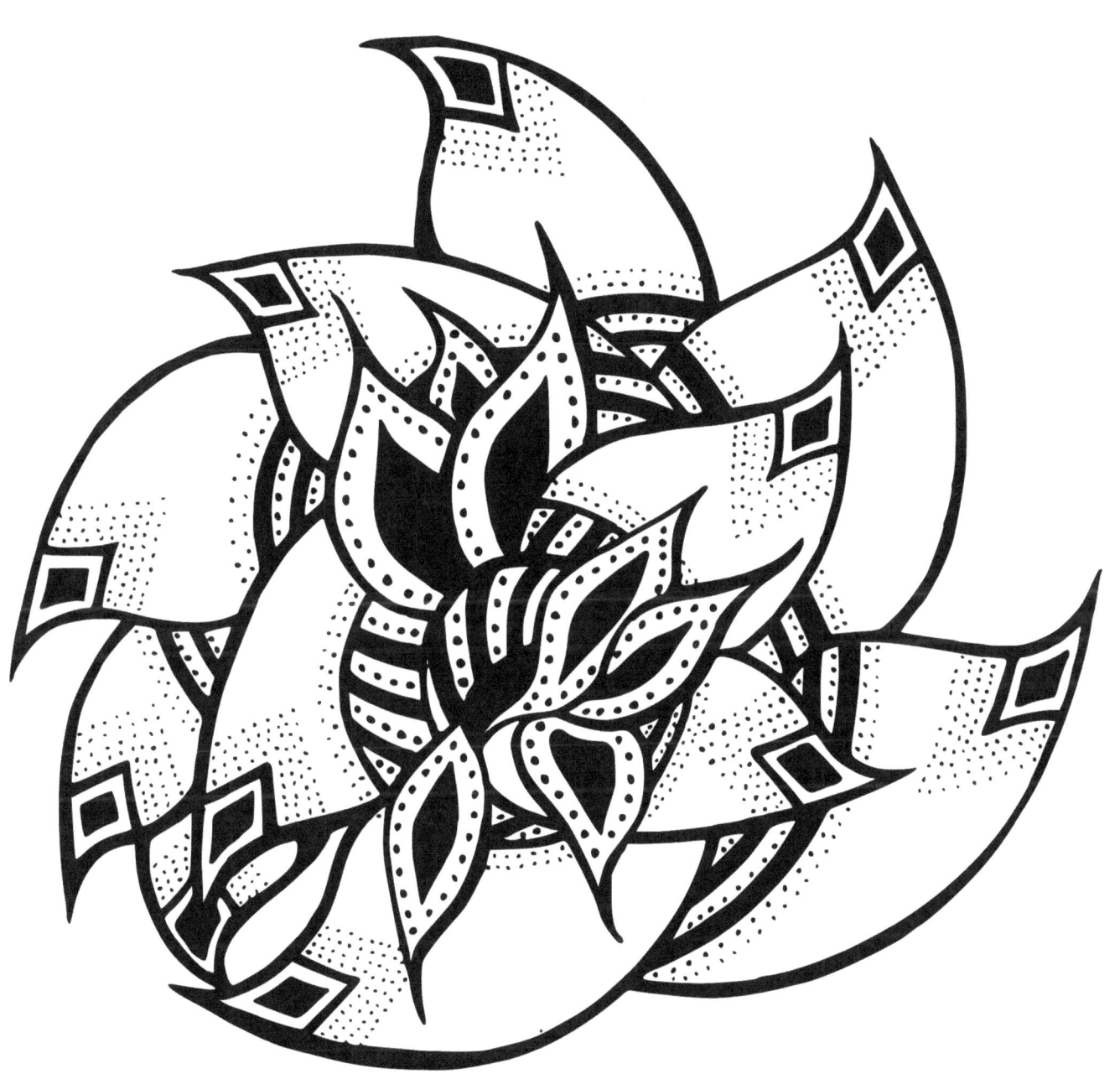

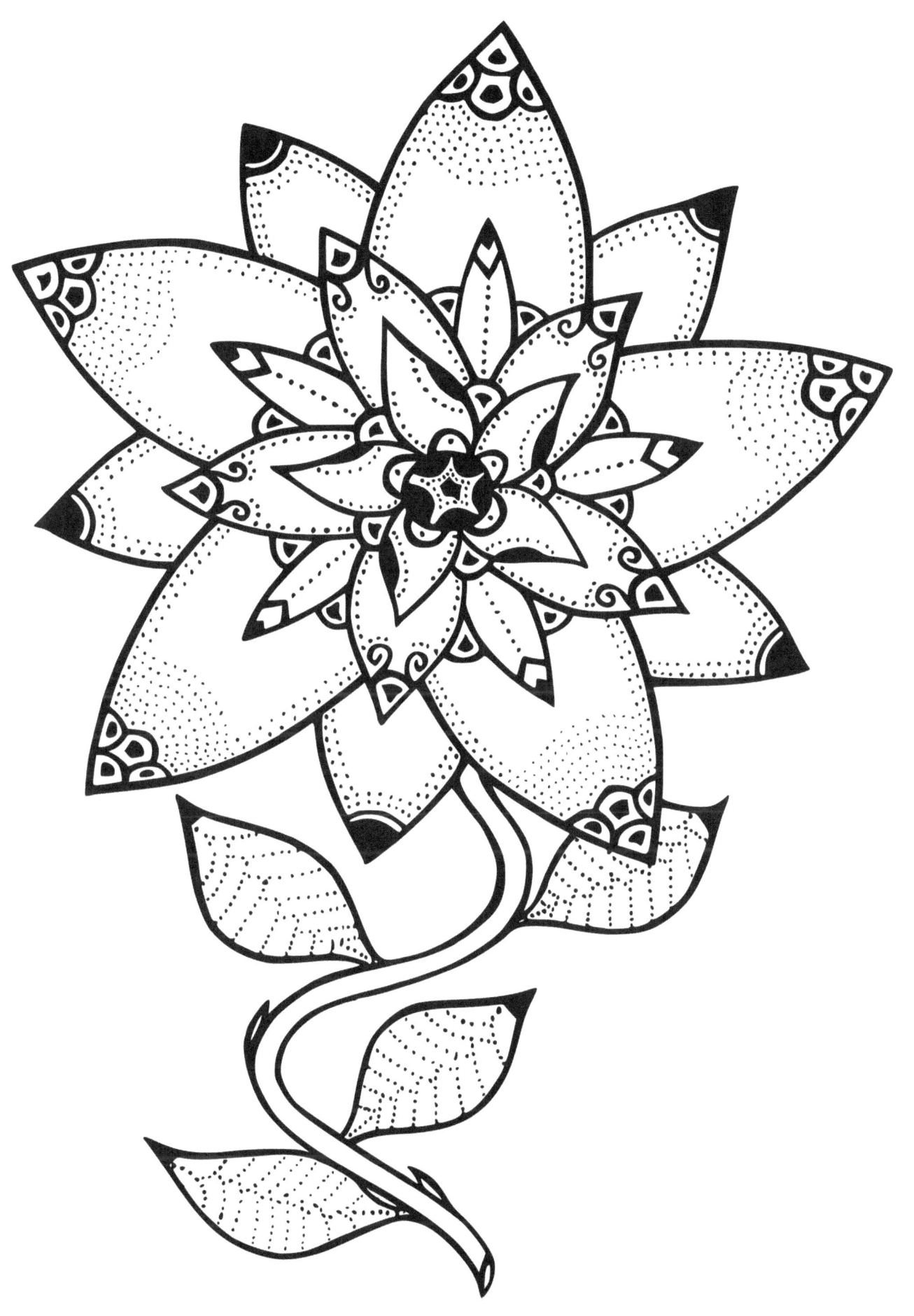

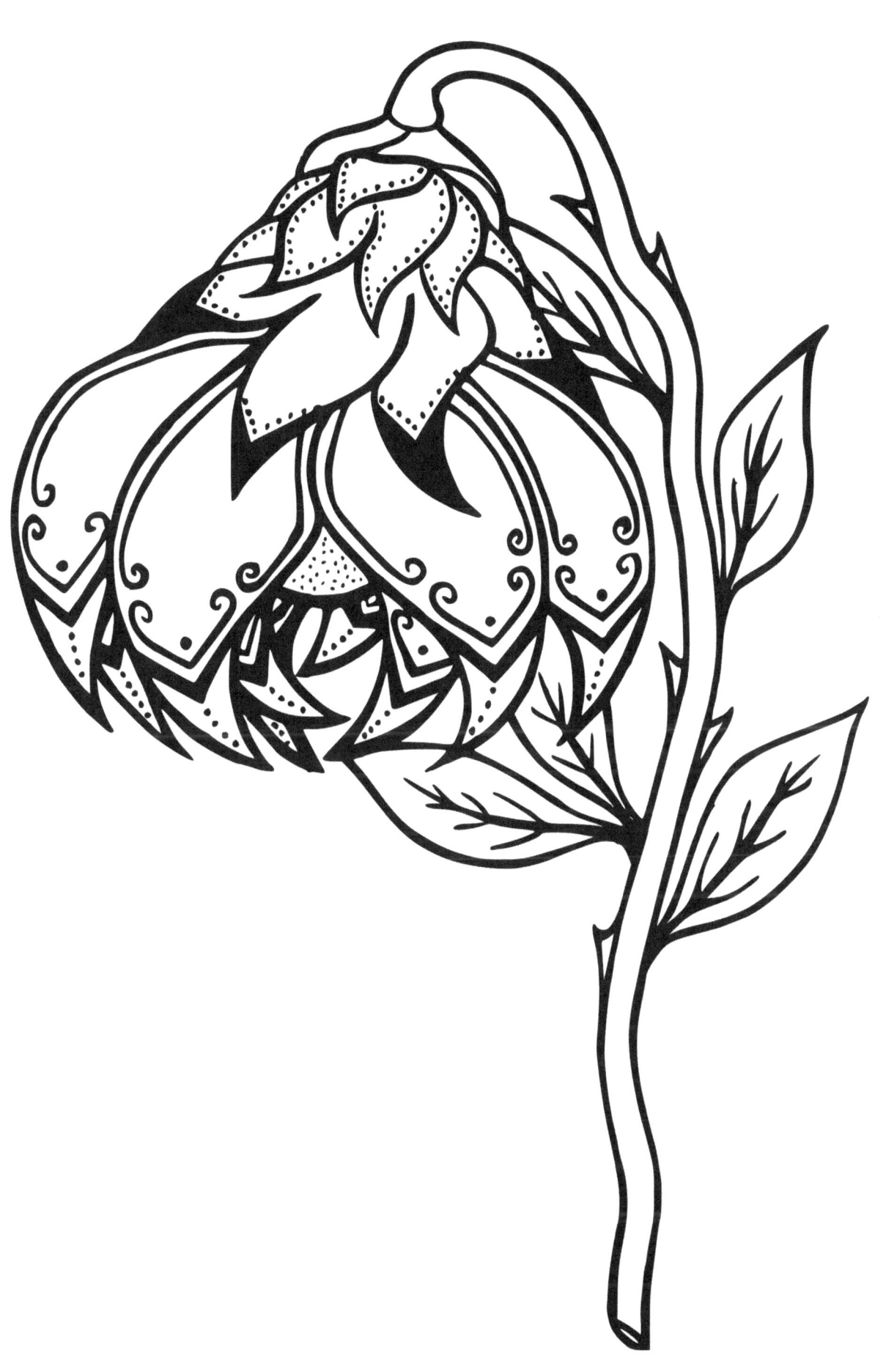

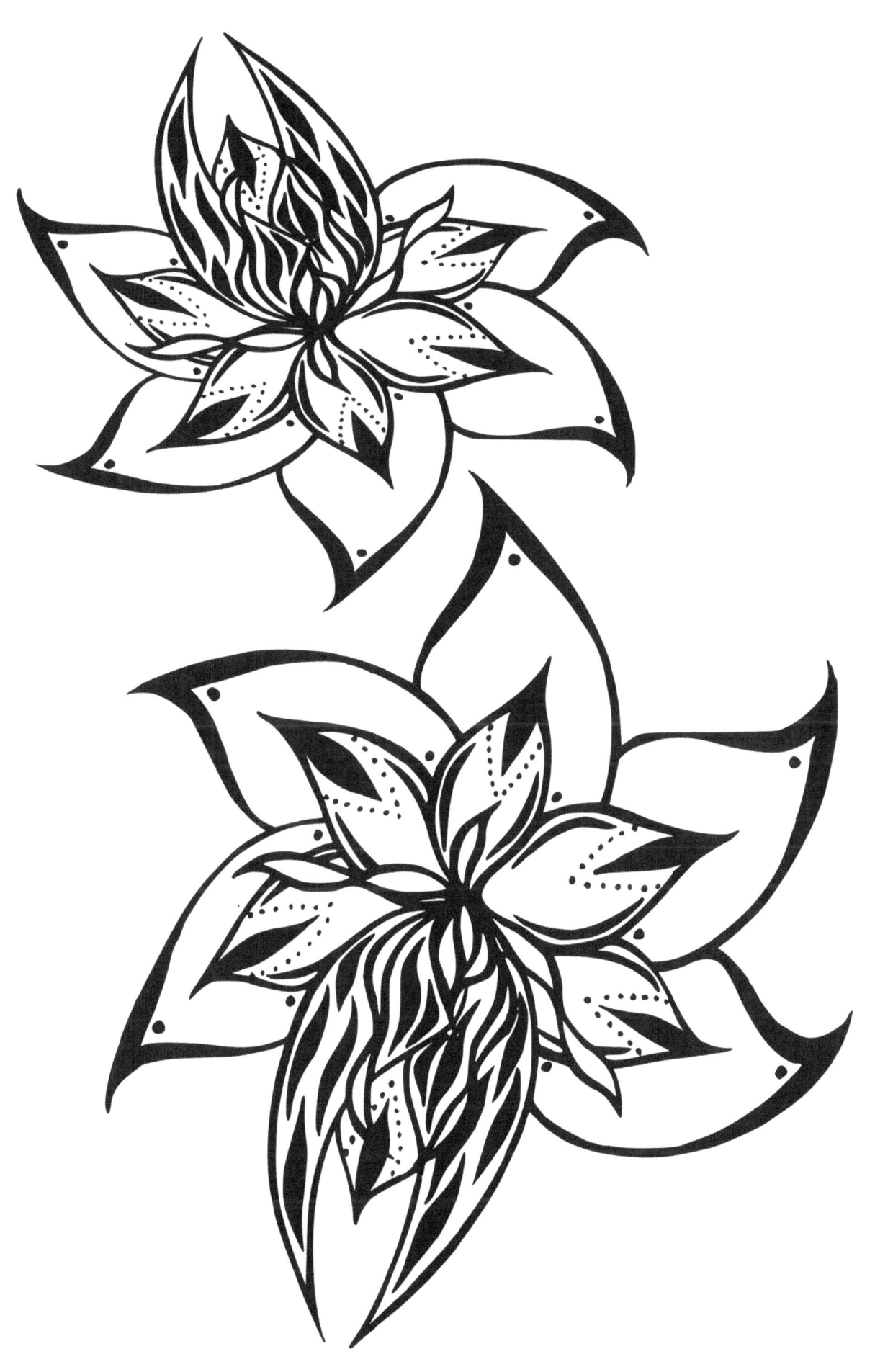

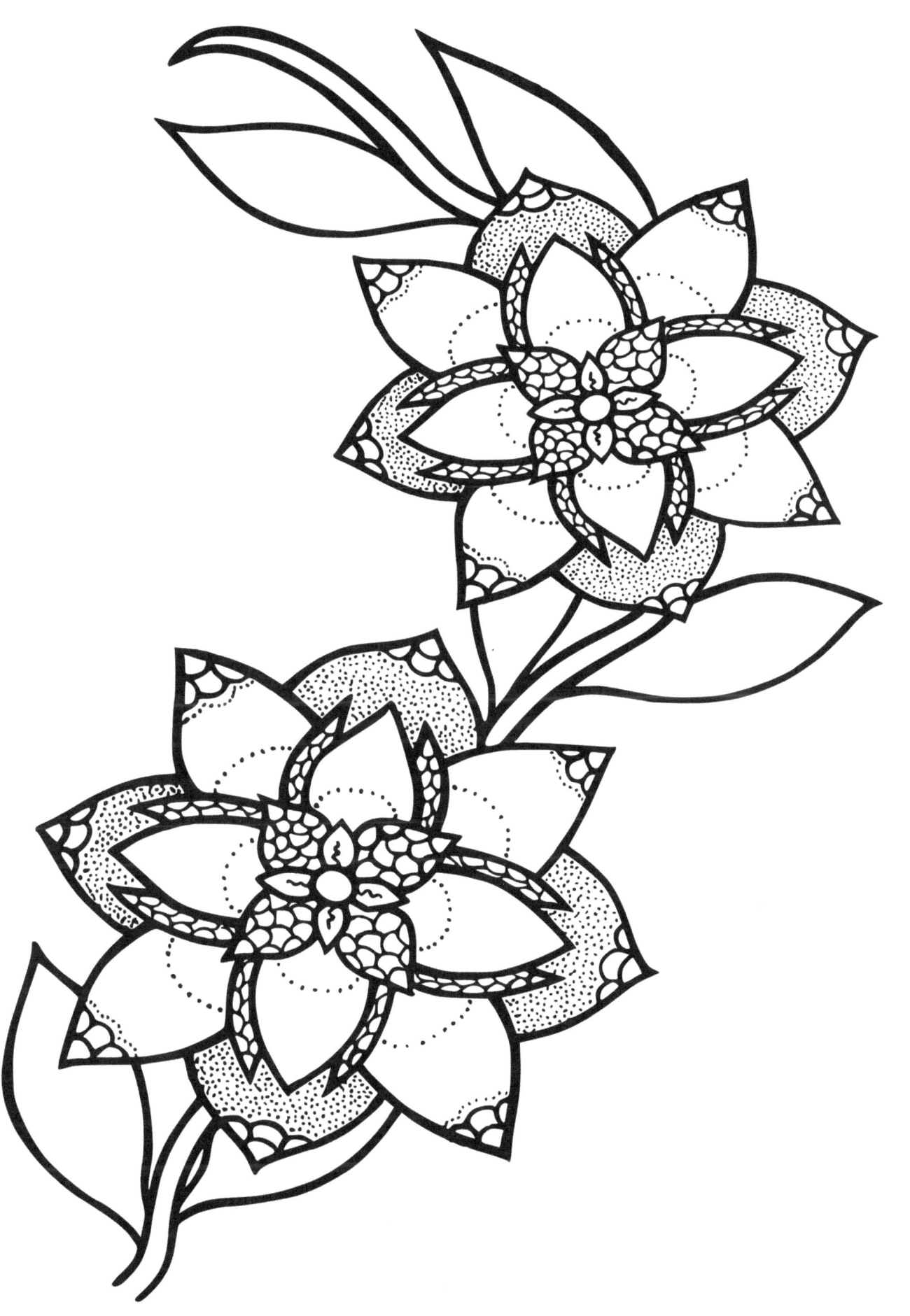

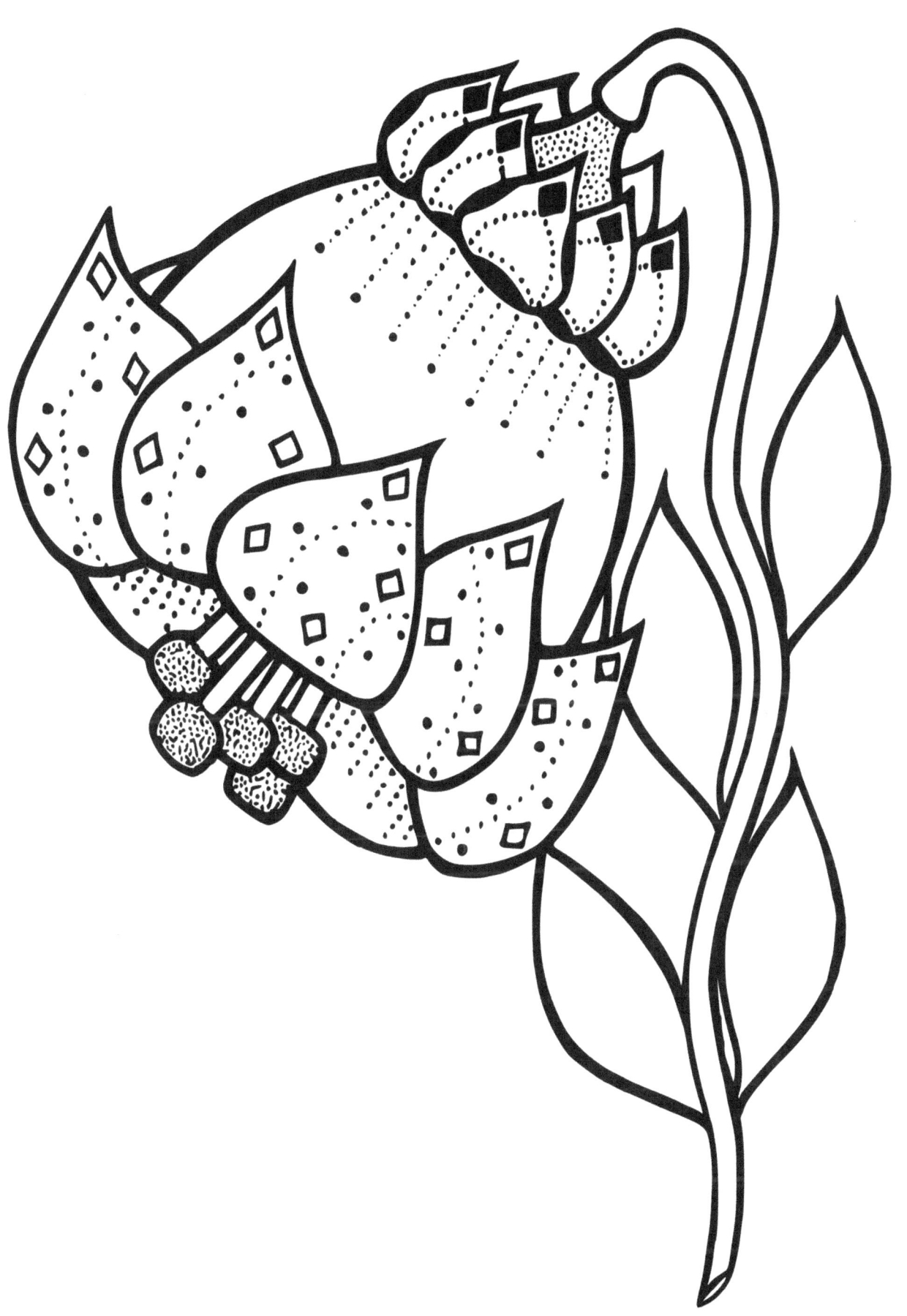

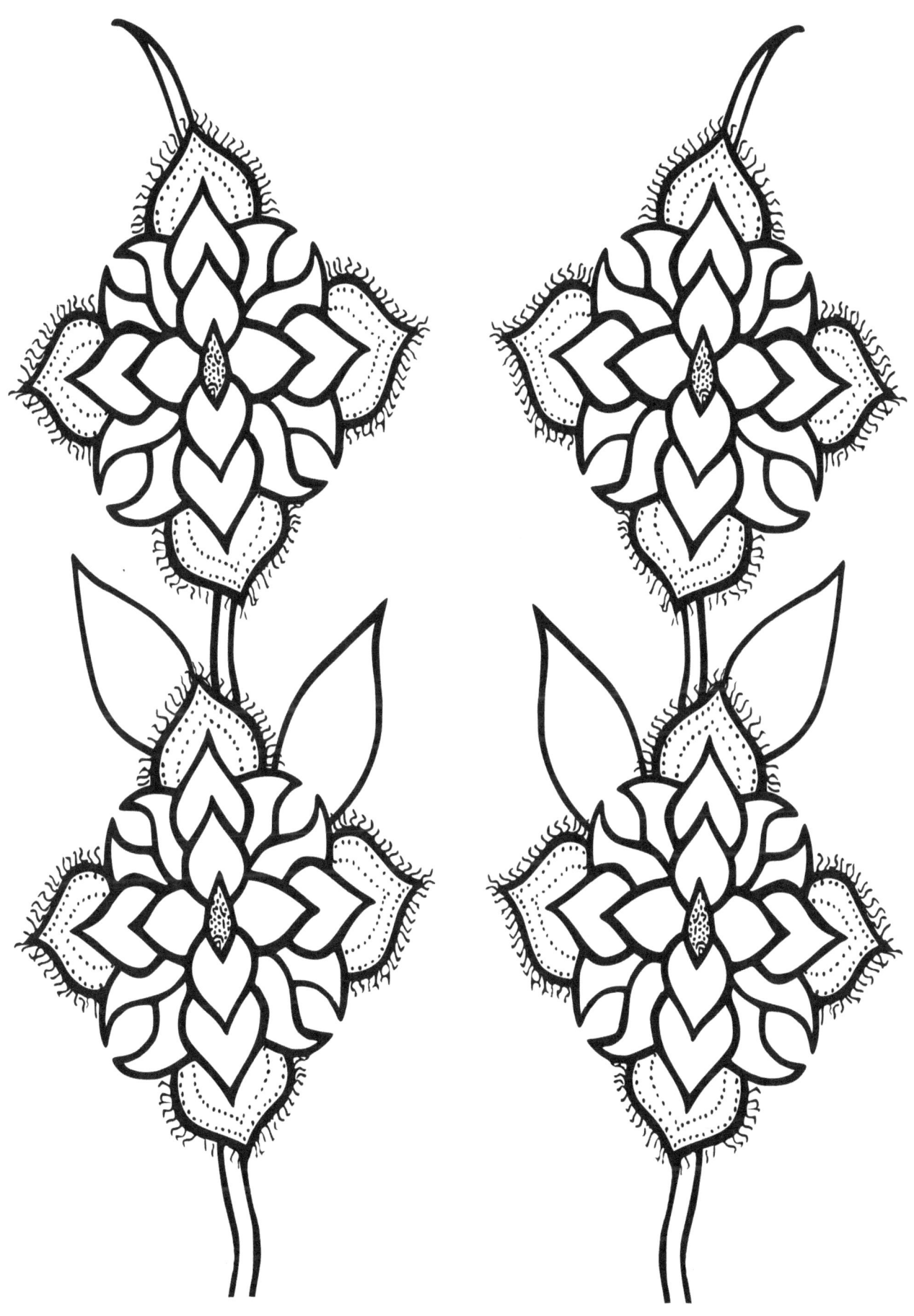

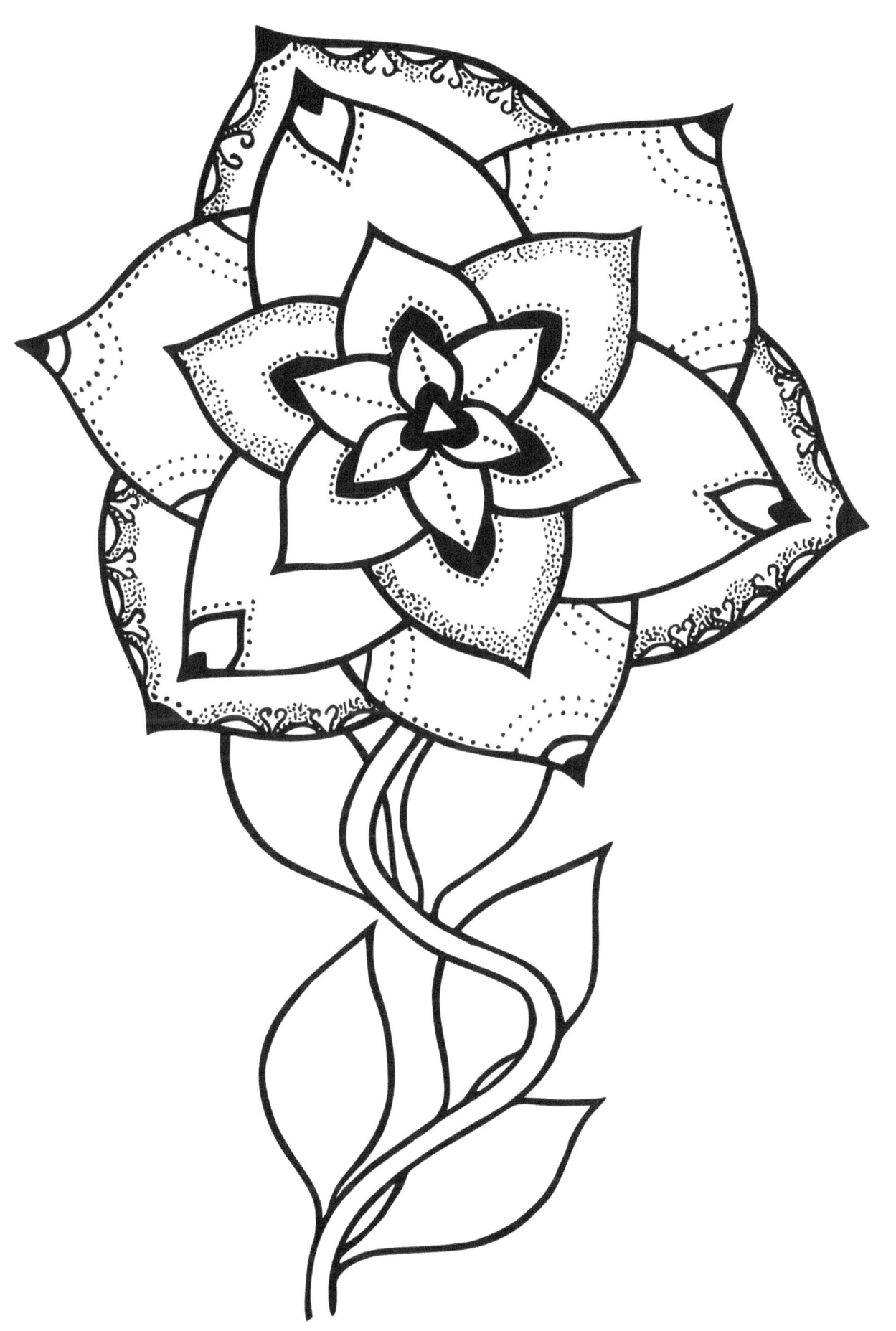

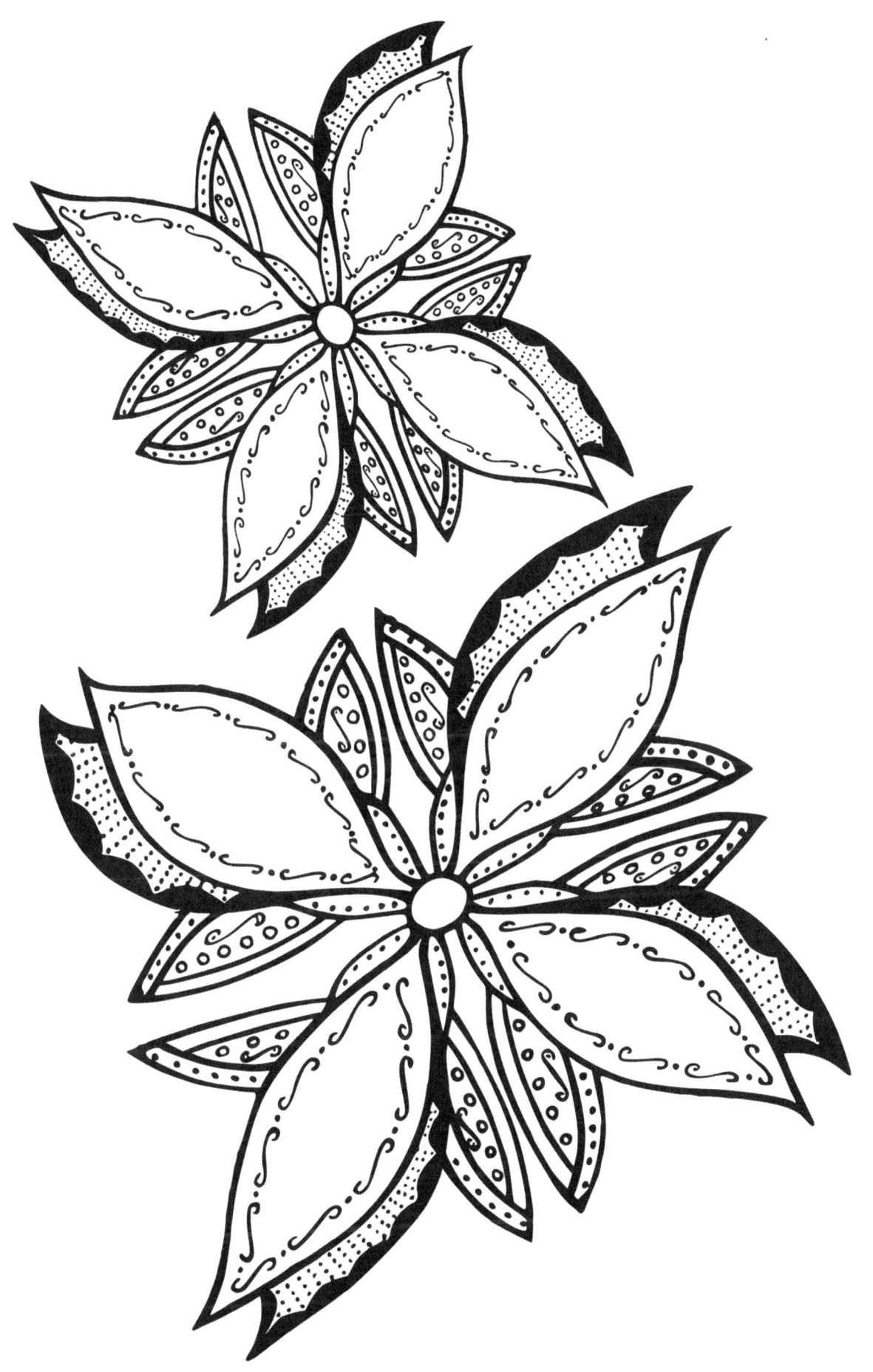

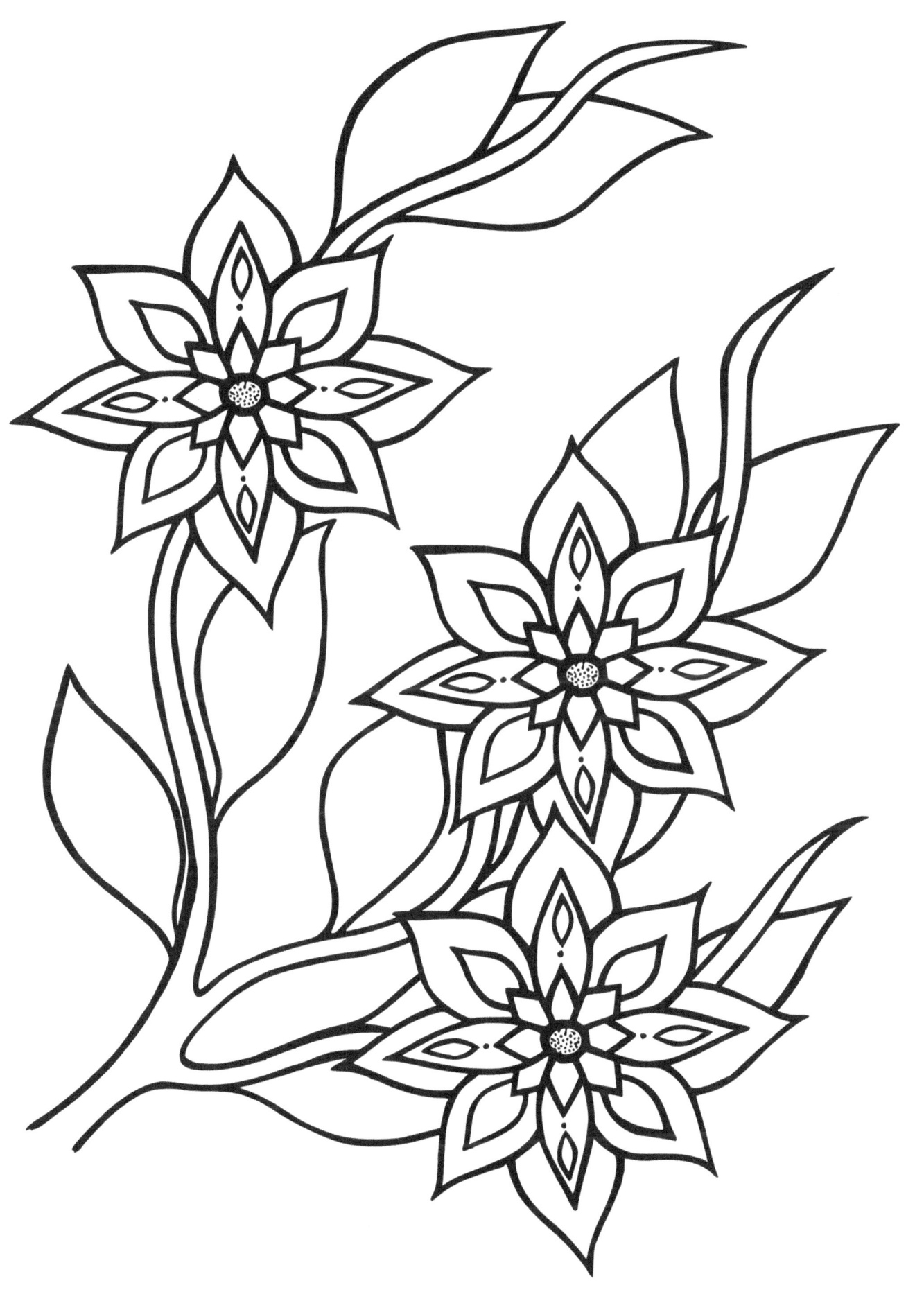

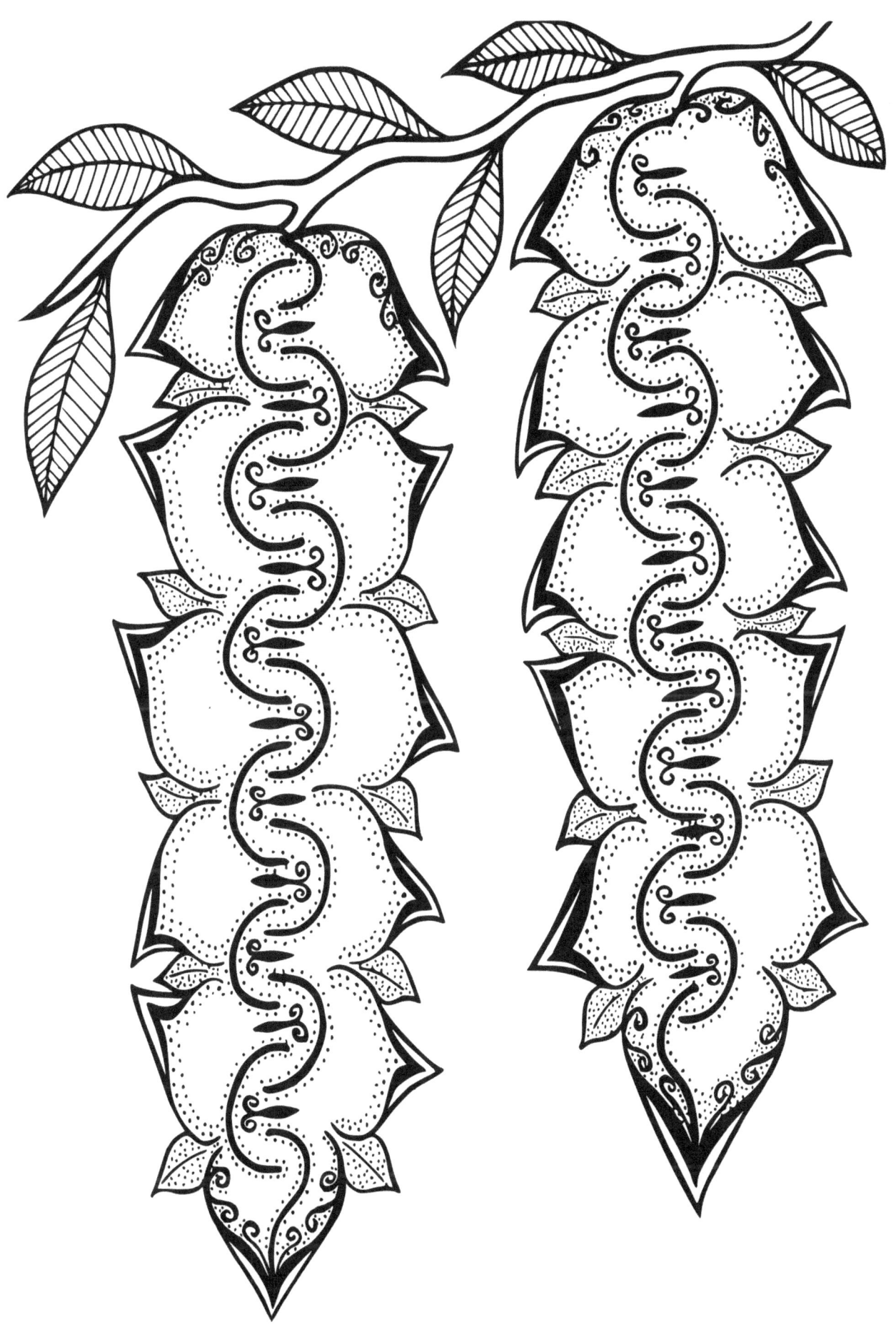

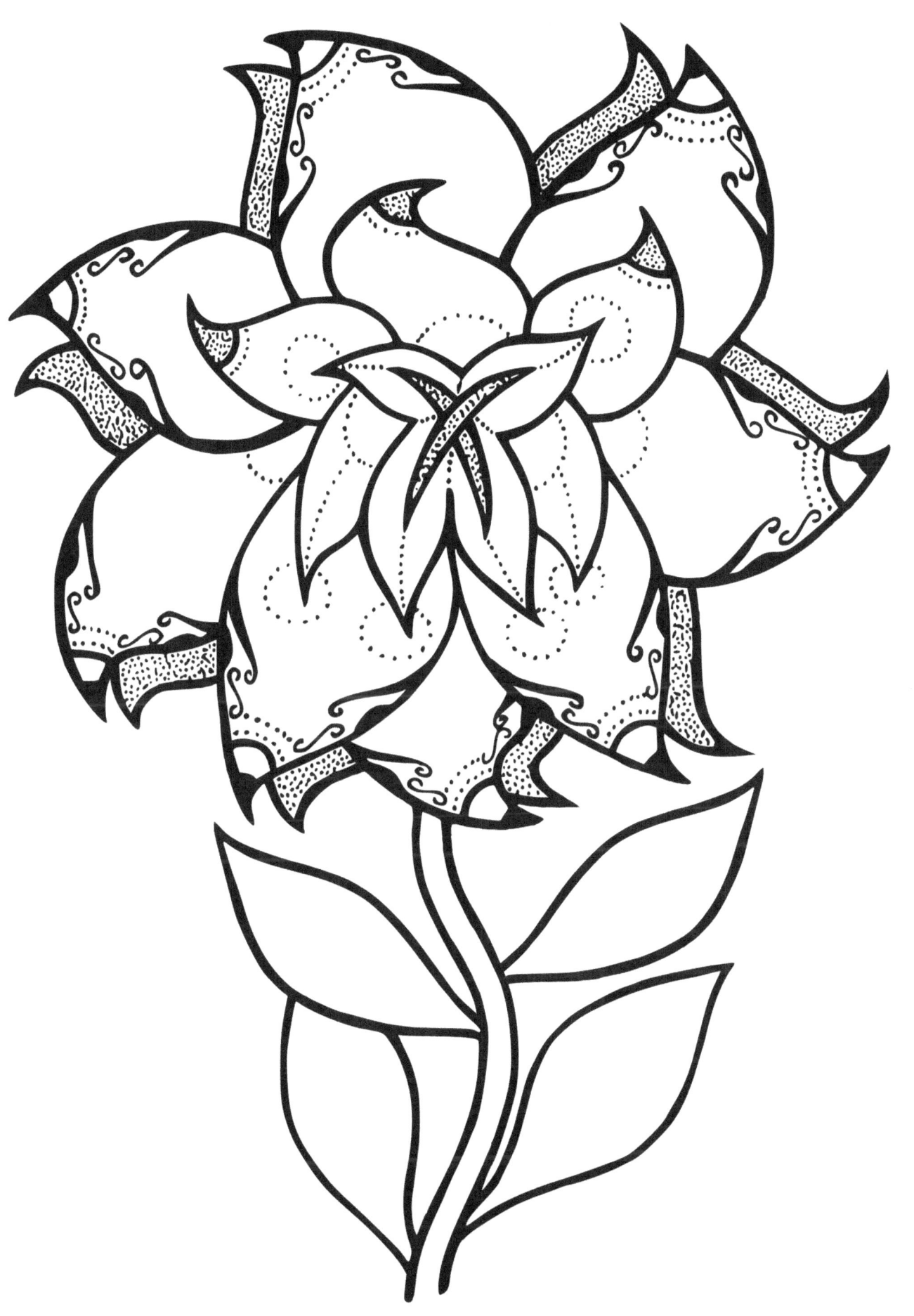

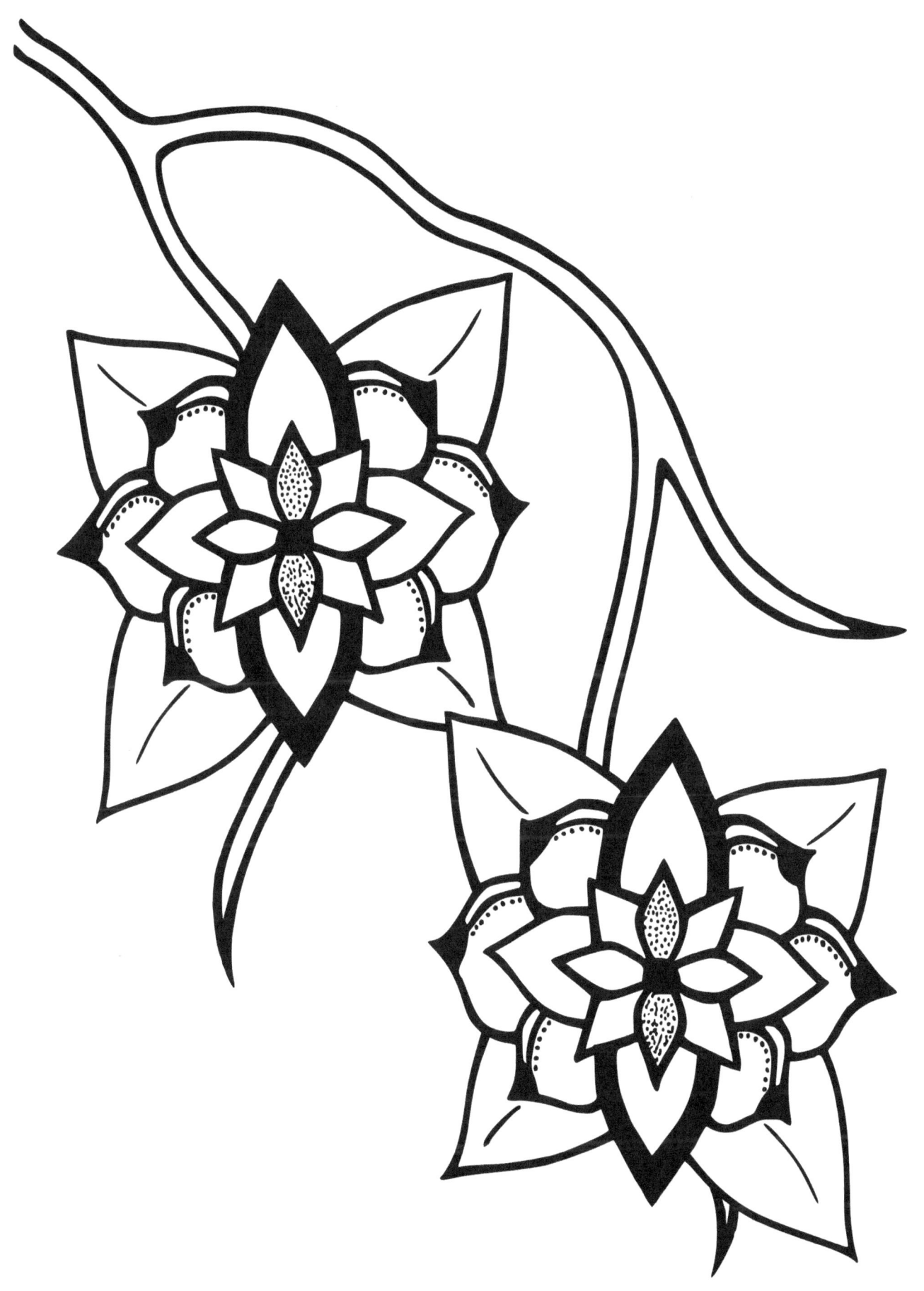

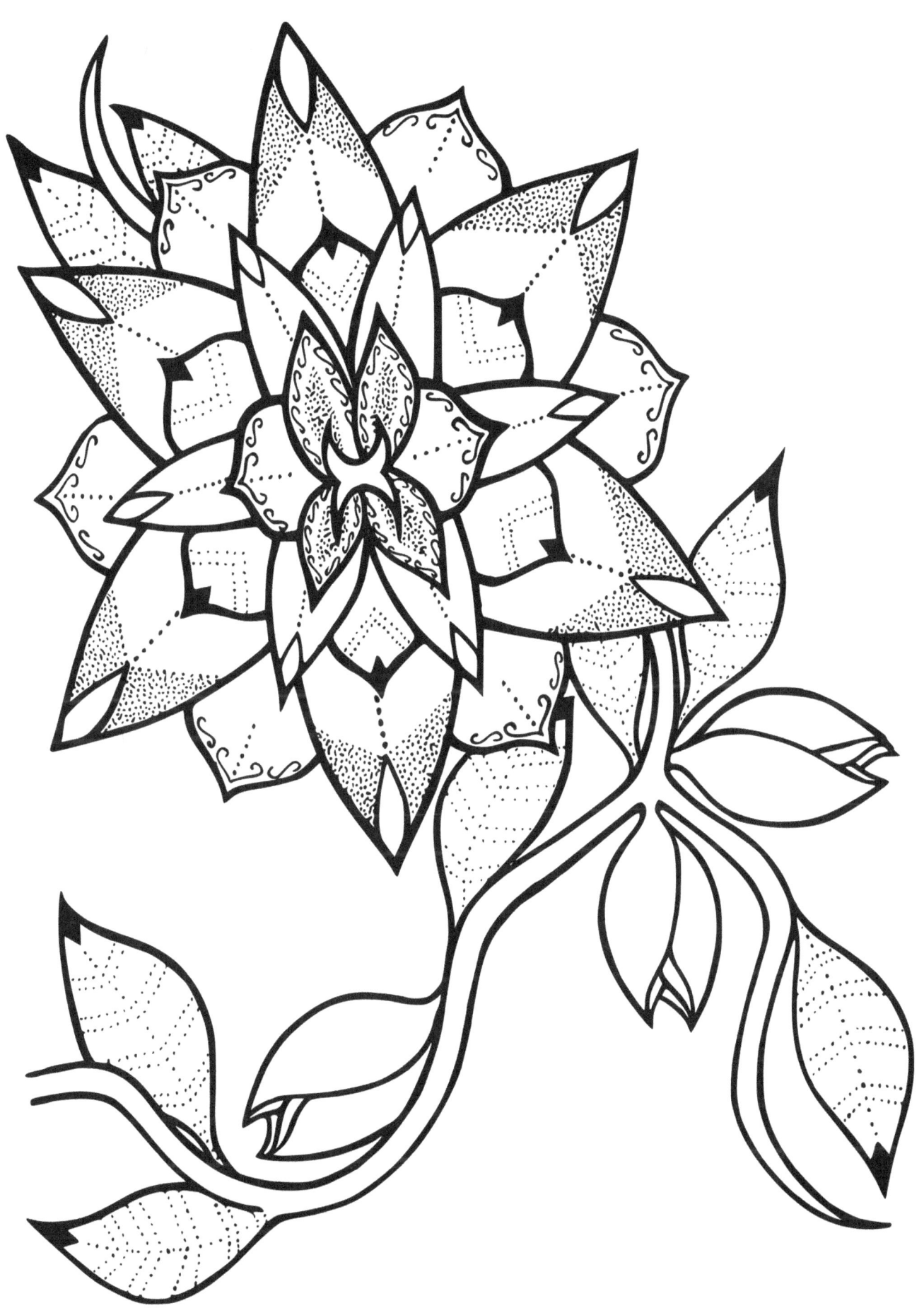

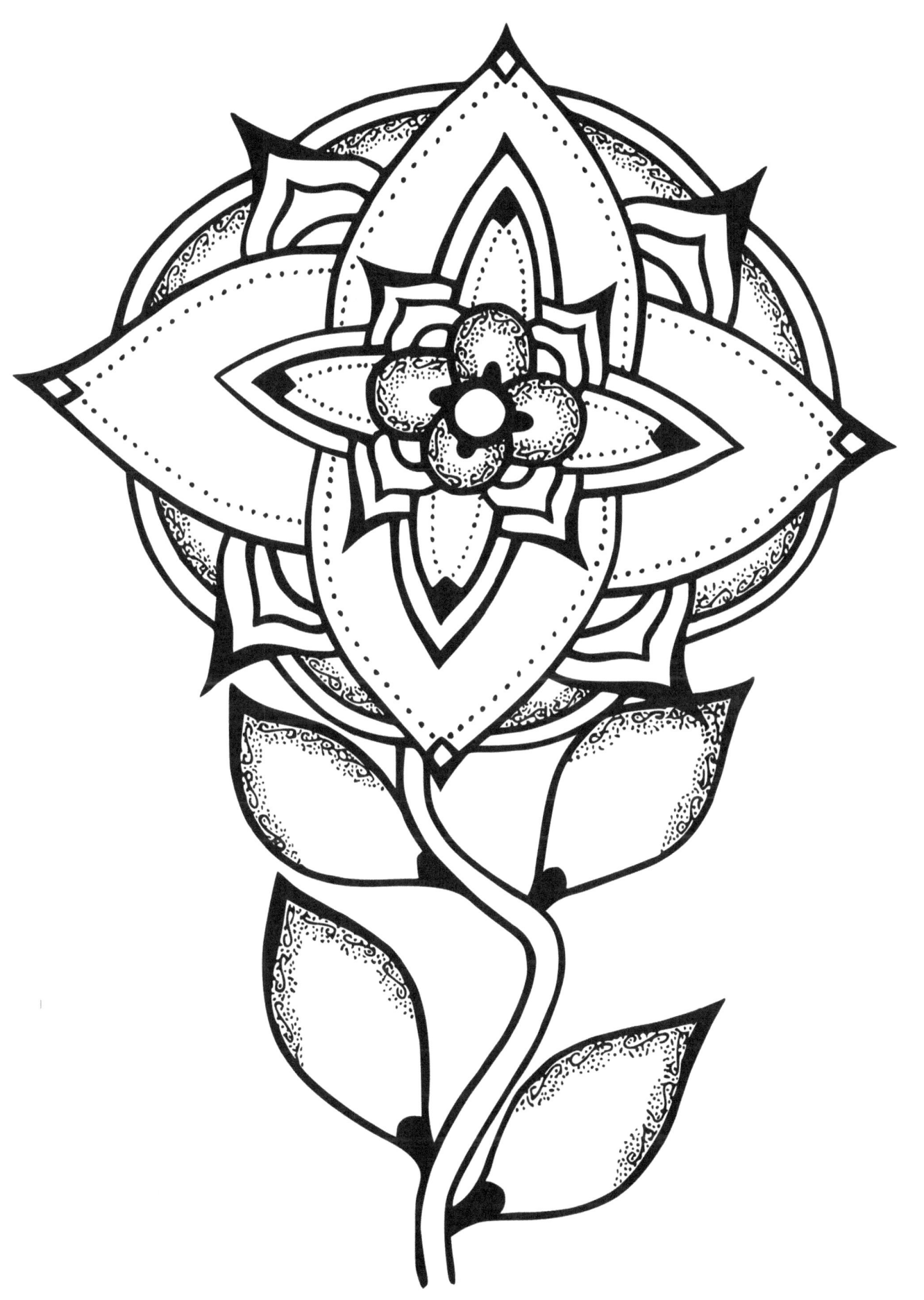

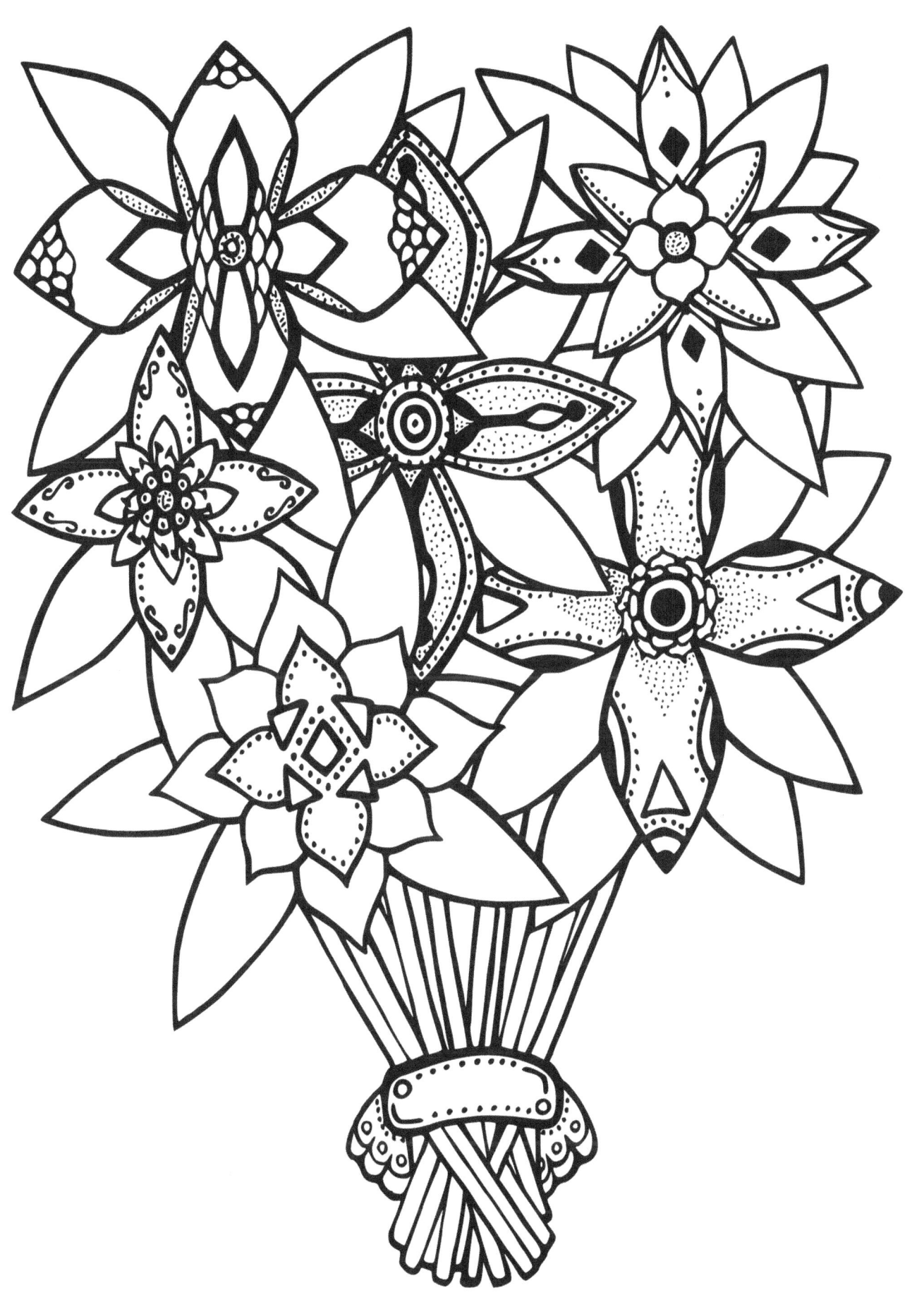

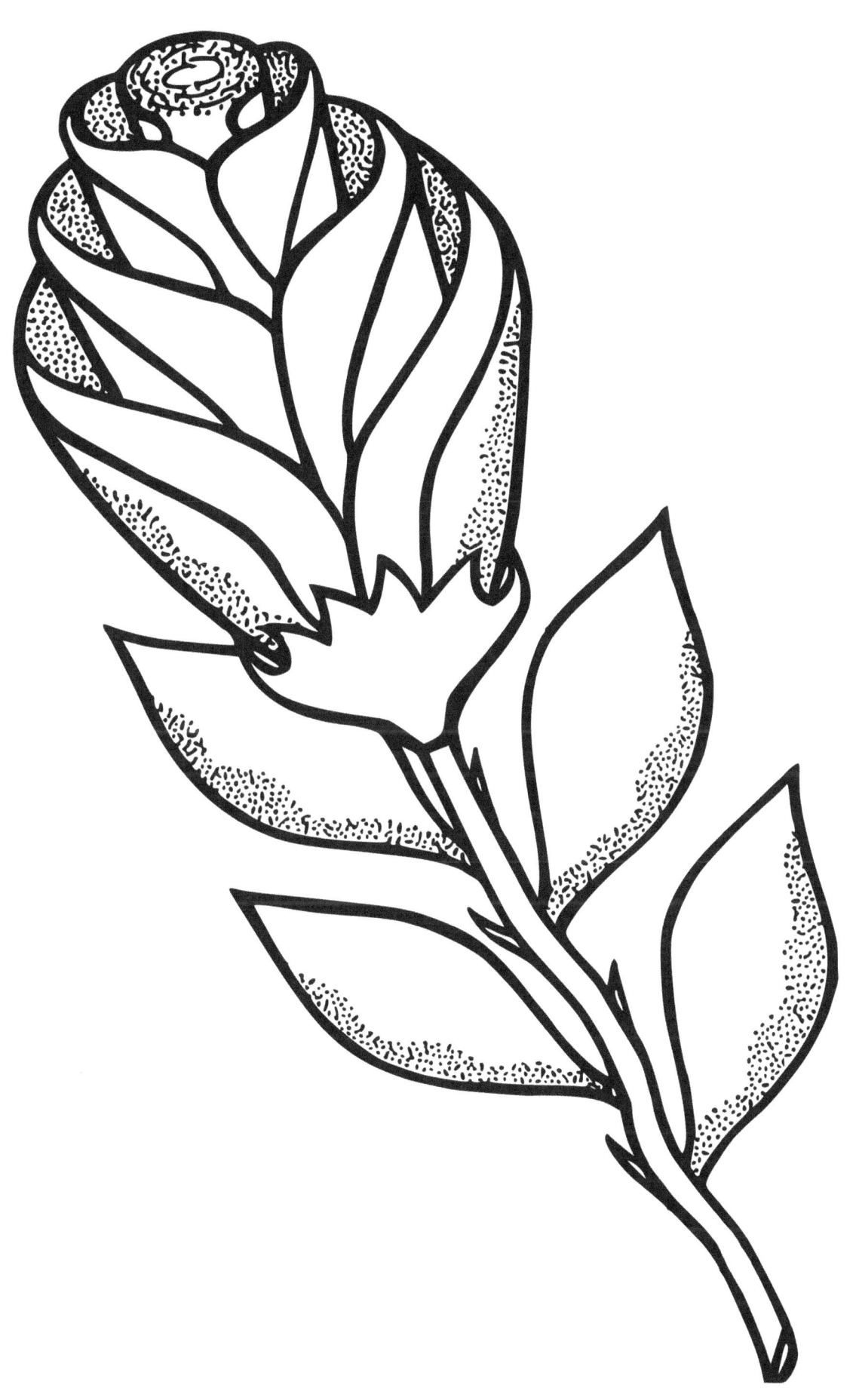